CONTENTS

UNIT 7 CONSTRUCTIONS AND PROJECTS   121

TO THE TEACHER

Who is this book for?

Drawing Out activities have been developed primarily for use in classes of English as a Second Language at junior high, secondary, adult, and junior college levels. Some activities may need slight modification depending on your students' background, age level, and language proficiency. And, naturally, it is always important to consider your own particular students' interests and experiences when choosing topics for discussion in the classroom. Not all topics here are extendable to every age group.

What is *Drawing Out*?

Drawing Out is a collection of acquisition activities that focus on student-created images as a means to becoming more communicative in the second language.

We do not assume that the students or their instructor are artists. Drawing Out activities are not intended to create an aesthetic product, though sometimes we are amazed at the creativity, the sensitivity, and the beauty of what is produced. Rather, student-created drawings are used as a means toward:

1. promoting clearer self-expression, especially during the early stages of language development;
2. allowing students to share a sense of personal or cultural identity with their classmates;

3. providing a focus or stimulus for oral interaction and written expression;
4. lowering tension;
5. building a feeling of empathy or community spirit through shared experience in the classroom;
6. having a good time together!

How do I implement the activities in this book?

The fifty-four topics in Units 1 through 6 require that pages be photocopied for use by the students. Students are given a subject to think about and are asked questions. They are instructed to draw a quick picture about that specific topic.

Before having students actually begin their drawings, you will want to discuss the topic with the group to make sure the focus is clear. Have students give you several examples orally. Share some ideas of your own. Sometimes you will want to begin the activity by providing a model — answering the question yourself with a scribble on the blackboard. Remember: if *your* drawings are not so well executed, so much the better. Students can laugh and relax, realizing that they are not necessarily trying to create something beautiful, but rather to give themselves something to talk or write about.

Give the students a time limit to finish their drawings — usually between five and eight minutes is sufficient, depending on the particular assignment. You will want them to work quickly, as the objective of the activity is the oral interaction that follows the drawing rather than the execution of the drawing itself.

Each activity asks that the students write something about their drawing. Some call only for labeling; others ask for sentence completion or short descriptions. Shorten or expand here to meet the needs and proficiency level of your particular group.

When the drawing and writing are completed, students sit down in groups of two to four. They show their drawings and read their writing to each other. Students who are more orally proficient are encouraged to ask questions about each other's work and continue the conversation for a set length of time.

Students who are at a higher level of language proficiency may then continue on to the second activity page that complements the drawing topic in some way. This second activity will be either a *Brainstorm!*, an *Interview!*, or a *Write About It!* assignment. It will require more extensive oral work with a partner or with a small group of classmates.

Most activities close with a volunteered sharing of the results of the activity with the whole class.

What is my role in *Drawing Out* activities?

As students are drawing, writing, and interacting, you will want to be circulating around the room from student to student, group to group, questioning, commenting, encouraging, joking, and inspiring students to become involved. This is your opportunity for one-to-one contact.

If possible, you will want to display student work on bulletin boards or in hallways for a time so that students will have an opportunity to read, look at, and comment on each other's work. You may also want to collect and photocopy entire sets of student work to make booklets to keep in the classroom for students to look through in their free time.

What sorts of materials will I need?

For the most part, you will want to use a large basket of crayons for all activities because **1)** they are inexpensive, and **2)** it is almost impossible to do beautiful drawings with crayons (thus lowering any student performance anxiety). Colored pencils or markers or just plain pencils are okay, too, depending on your school budget. You may discover that students will start bringing their own fancy-colored marking pens, once they become accustomed to the drawing idea!

Activities in Units 1 through 6 require only photocopied pages and something with which to draw.

The activities in Unit 7 do not require duplicated pages for the students. These tasks are more manipulative and constructive in nature. Students are asked to tear up magazines, cut, paste, draw, and make collages, posters, murals, and the like. Many of these activities are carried out by pairs or groups of students rather than individuals. Unit 7 activities will require such things as scissors, construction paper, glue sticks or rubber cement, index cards, large pieces of butcher paper or chart paper, and, sometimes, stacks of old magazines. No written instructions are handed out to the students; complete instructions for each activity in Unit 7 are given within the unit.

How will my students respond to drawing activities?

You know your own personal teaching style. We assume you are a creative, curious, adventuresome teacher who wants to explore all successful teaching modes, or you wouldn't have this book in your hand! Still, we know that teachers are hesitant about approaching new methods because they are not sure how students will react. You can already comfortably predict how your students will react to text exercises, oral group drills, pattern practice, and dictations. Both you and your students have done these things for a long time. But, then, maybe that is why you are exploring *Drawing Out.*

In our personal experience, at the secondary, adult, and junior college level, we have seen only positive responses to drawing activities. Each activity in this book has been successfully implemented many times. (The not-so-successful ones we have left out, you will be glad to know!)

Of course, on occasion, we will have one or two students who are less than enthusiastic when first confronted with the opportunity to draw, even as a brief alternative to analytic text and workbook tasks. There will always be students (and teachers!) who resist or reject any sort of unusual or unfamiliar classroom activity. We have learned to avoid and prepare for these negative student reactions so that all students feel free to participate. If this is a concern to you, the following are some guidelines to consider:

1. Ask your students about their past language-learning experiences. Find out what their expectations are. What sort of classroom activity have they done before to learn language? How helpful was it to them?

2. Use language teaching strategies that they are *familiar with* and *expect to begin with*. Validate their past experience. Do what "real" teachers do.

3. Communicate your personal expertise from the very first moment— your "years" of experience, your competence, the success of past students. Show them in subtle ways that you have a lot of effective ideas. Gain their confidence in you by showing them their daily success and progress in your classroom. If they feel successful with you, they will try anything!

4. Take time to get acquainted first! Students need to know who you are and they need to know each other before trying "risky" strategies. Where there is friendship, there is more trust, less fear of embarrassment or failure.

5. Learn about the students' values, interests, and concerns, so that the topics you choose for drawing and discussion are motivating and relevant to their model of the world.

6. Gradually implement these activities. Do short, safe, easy ones first. The more success initially, the less resistance later.

7. If absolutely necessary, offer the choice of other solo tasks for those one or two students who are initially resistant to new strategies. Forcing or coercing participation obviously serves no pedagogical purpose. Offer a fill-in sheet or a short reading activity to the resistant student to complete while the rest of the class continues as planned. Rarely will a student choose to work apart after witnessing the jolly, friendly, oral / social interaction that is a result of these activities.

8. Create a poster that you can leave up in your classroom that lists reasons why you plan drawing activities as a part of language learning. Remind the students from time to time of these objectives. Example:

We Are Drawing in this Classroom to:
- Practice expressing ourselves
- Show people who we are
- Listen and learn about other people
- Leave the text and workbook for awhile
- Have something to write about or talk about
- Learn new ideas from other people
- Have fun!

You have known all along that language input is *received* aurally, visually, and kinesthetically. As you put these activities into practice in your classroom, you will also see how much output may be *formulated* and *produced* when students are allowed kinesthetic and visual expressive modes.

Language is all confrontation and experimentation. We hope that you and your learners enjoy and benefit from this addition to the lesson plan as much as we have!

UNIT **1**

FRIENDS AND FAMILY

My Best Friend

Who is your best friend here in the United States? Draw a picture of your best friend.

WRITE ABOUT YOUR DRAWING

My best friend's name is _____.

I met my friend in _____.

He/She is _____.

He/She likes _____.

Together we _____.

The best thing about her/him is _____

_____.

Share your drawing and sentences with your classmates. Tell more about your best friend.

BRAINSTORM!

Sit down in groups of four. Look at this picture. This person is the **ideal friend**—the **perfect companion.** Together with your partners, make a list of all the things about this person that make her such a good friend. What kind of person is she? What does she do that shows her friendship?

FIFTEEN QUALITIES OF A GOOD FRIEND

1. _____
2. _____
3. _____
4. _____
5. _____
6. _____
7. _____
8. _____
9. _____
10. _____
11. _____
12. _____
13. _____
14. _____
15. _____

When you have finished your list, share your ideas orally with the whole class. Are your ideas very similar or very different? The teacher will make a poster of your ideas to remind you of what it means to be a good friend.

DRAWING OUT © 1992 by Prentice-Hall, Inc.
Permission granted to reproduce for classroom use.

Family Tree

This family tree is a picture of your close family members. Draw **your** face in the large circle. Draw your brothers on the left and your sisters on the right. Draw your mother and father *over* your picture. If you are married, draw your wife or husband *under* your picture and your children, too.

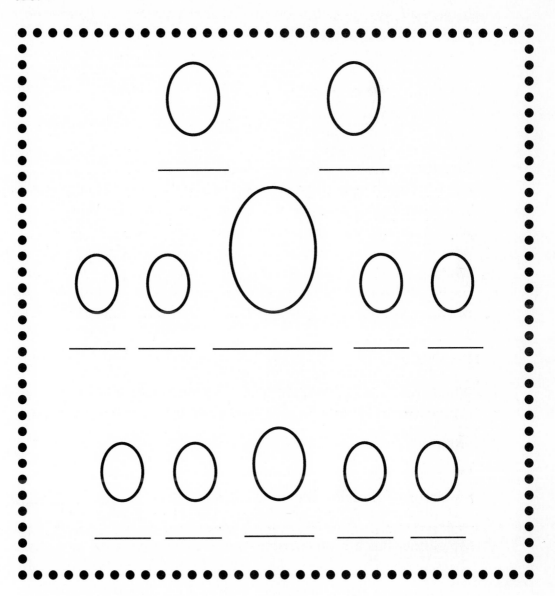

WRITE ABOUT YOUR DRAWING

Under each picture, write the names and ages of your family members.

Share your family tree pictures and names with your classmates. Tell more about your family.

INTERVIEW!

Sit down with a partner. Ask your partner the questions in Part 1 below. Listen very carefully. When you are finished with the interview, thank your partner. Then your partner will ask you the questions.

If there are any questions on the list that you or your partner do not want to answer, say "I pass on that question."

When both partners have been interviewed, write the answers to the questions in Part 2. If you can't remember, it is okay to ask your partner again!

PART 1

How many brothers and sisters do you have?

Are your brothers and sisters living here in this city? If not, where are they?

Which brother or sister do you think is very special? Why?

What is something your family likes (or liked) to do together?

Who is the boss in your family? How do you know that person is the boss?

When you were a child, did you ever make your parents angry? If yes, what did you do to make them angry?

Did your father ever teach you how to do something? If yes, what did he teach you?

Did your parents have "rules" that you had to follow? If yes, tell me about one rule they had for you.

When you have children will you raise them with the same rules your parents had for you? Or will you raise them very differently?

PART 2

My partner has _____ brothers and _____ sisters.

My partner's brothers and sisters live in _____

_____.

My partner has a brother/sister who is special because _____

_____.

Something the family likes (or liked) to do together is _____

_____.

In my partner's family, the _____ is the boss.

One rule my partner's parents had was _____

_____.

When you are finished, trade papers with your partner to make sure it is accurate. Make any necessary changes, then return the paper.

DRAWING OUT © 1992 by Prentice-Hall, Inc. Permission granted to reproduce for classroom use.

A Gift Box for My Family

This is a magic gift box! Any kind of present you want to give to your family—large or small—will fit in this little box. Draw a picture of the special present you would like to give to your family in this magic box!

WRITE ABOUT YOUR DRAWING

I want to give my family _____

because _____.

Share your drawing and sentences with your classmates. Tell more about the present you want to give your family.

WRITE ABOUT IT!

With your partner, read the following questions. Discuss together which solution you think is the best choice for each problem. Make up a completely different solution if you don't like the choices given to you.

PROBLEM 1

Your mother, who lives with you, has given you a book for your birthday. You know she spent a lot of time choosing just the right book for you. It is **not** a book you are interested in. But there **is** another book you really want. You know you could exchange it at the bookstore very easily for the one you want. What do you do?

___ **1.** Keep the book your mother gave you.

___ **2.** Trade the book for the other one and hope your mother doesn't know.

___ **3.** Thank your mother for the book and tell her that you would really like a different one and want to exchange it.

PROBLEM 2

You have a new friend. He is very rich. On your birthday, he gave you a watch that you know costs over $200. You like this watch **very much**, but you feel very uncomfortable keeping such an expensive gift. You don't know why he gave you such an expensive gift. You could never spend so much for a gift for him. What do you do?

___ **1.** Say "Thank you" and keep the gift.

___ **2.** Return the gift, saying "I really like the watch, but it is just too expensive. I don't feel right about keeping it."

___ **3.** You keep the watch and then save money to buy a similar gift for him on his birthday.

After you talk about your choices and listen to your partner's ideas, write about what you would probably do to solve these problems.

_____

_____

_____

_____

_____

_____

_____

DRAWING OUT © 1992 by Prentice-Hall, Inc.
Permission granted to reproduce for classroom use.

Talking with Your Best Friend

Who is your best friend? What do you talk about with your best friend? Draw your face and your best friend's face.

WRITE ABOUT YOUR PICTURE

What do you say to your best friend? What does your best friend say to you? In the balloons, write a conversation between you and your friend.

Share your drawing and writing with your classmates. Tell more about your conversations with your best friend.

WRITE ABOUT IT!

Sit down in groups of four. Together look at these people. They are new neighbors and possible new friends for you. Tell your partners which person you would choose for your new friend and why you would choose that person.

He rides a motorcycle. His idea of fun is to go to loud noisy parties with a lot of other people and stay out late at night. He loves rock-and-roll music; his favorite dinner is hamburgers and french fries. He is an automobile mechanic and works hard. He goes to church every Sunday. He loves his family and is a very happy man.

He is a very quiet, thoughtful person. He likes to read and to listen to soft music. He writes poetry. His favorite evening out is to go to a classical music concert or a foreign film. He likes long, philosophical conversations with one or two close friends. He is a vegetarian. He has no family and, at the moment, he has no job.

He likes the outdoors. He goes camping once a month and loves to hike in the mountains. He is a real athlete. He gets up at six o'clock every morning and runs five miles. He hates to dress up in formal clothes. He has four dogs. He was married two times, but now he is divorced. He works in construction. He has a lot of money.

Now that you have decided which person you would choose for a friend, write about your reasons. Are you similar to that person or very different? What do you have in common? What do you find especially interesting about the person? Is he like another friend you have?

_____

_____

_____

_____

_____

DRAWING OUT © 1992 by Prentice-Hall, Inc.
Permission granted to reproduce for classroom use.

My Family

You have a special family. Who is *one* person in your family who is very special to you—a brother, an uncle, your mother? Draw a picture of your special family member.

WRITE ABOUT YOUR DRAWING

Who is this special person in your family? What does this person look like? What kind of person is he or she? What do you especially love about this person?

_____

_____

_____

_____

_____

_____

Share your drawing and your sentences with your classmates. Tell more about this special family member. Show a photo if you have one.

WRITE ABOUT IT!

Sit down in a group of four. You are all brothers and sisters. You are 8, 11, 14, and 17 years old. You live with your parents. You love your parents very much. They are very good to you. But sometimes they make you very unhappy. Sometimes you think they just don't understand you. Sometimes they are not very fair. Together, talk about the things your parents do or say to you that **you appreciate**. Write a list. Then talk about the things your parents do or say that **make you crazy** and write a list!

We appreciate our parents because they. . .

1. _____
2. _____
3. _____
4. _____
5. _____
6. _____
7. _____
8. _____

Our parents make us angry when they. . .

1. _____
2. _____
3. _____
4. _____
5. _____
6. _____
7. _____
8. _____

When you finish making your lists, share your ideas with the whole class. Are your ideas similar or different?

DRAWING OUT © 1992 by Prentice-Hall, Inc.
Permission granted to reproduce for classroom use.

Pets—Our Other Friends

Do you have a pet? A dog? A cat? A bird? Or did you have a pet before? Draw a picture of a pet you have or had in your family.

WRITE ABOUT YOUR DRAWING

What is your pet? What does it look like? Is it big or small? What color is it? What do you like about this pet? What special things can this pet do?

_____

_____

_____

_____

_____

Share your drawing and your sentences with your classmates. Tell more about your pet.

BRAINSTORM!

Sit down in a group of four. Many people in the United States have a dog or a cat for a pet. Some people have birds or fish or small turtles as pets. You are a family that has decided to adopt a pet. But only two animals are available—a large, black, friendly spider and a sheep. Discuss with your "family" what would be good or nice about having each animal for a pet. Then discuss the problems of having them for pets. Write a list of the "pros" and "cons."

THE SPIDER

The big, black spider would be a **good** pet because. . .

1. _____
2. _____
3. _____
4. _____

The spider might **not** be a good pet because. . .

1. _____
2. _____
3. _____
4. _____

THE SHEEP

The sheep would be a **good** pet because. . .

1. _____
2. _____
3. _____
4. _____

The sheep might **not** be a good pet because. . .

1. _____
2. _____
3. _____
4. _____

When you are finished, share your ideas orally with the whole class.

14

Activities with Friends

What do you like *to do* with your friends? Where do you *go* with them? Draw a picture of you and two of your friends. Where are you and what are you doing?

WRITE ABOUT YOUR DRAWING

With my friends, I like to _____

_____

_____.

Sometimes, we _____

_____

_____.

Share your drawing and sentences with your classmates. Tell more about your activities with friends.

BRAINSTORM!

Sit down in a group of four. Do you ever get bored? Do you ever just sit down and not have any ideas of what to do for fun? If our friends are around us we can usually find something fun or interesting to do, but it is more difficult when we are alone. With your group members, brainstorm a list of things that are fun to do—in your town or in your own home—when you are alone. Write as many ideas as you can think of.

1. Bake cookies.
2. Exercise in your living room.
3. Ride a bicycle.
4. _____
5. _____
6. _____
7. _____
8. _____
9. _____
10. _____
11. _____
12. _____
13. _____
14. _____
15. _____

When you are finished with your list, share your ideas orally with the whole class. How many ideas does the class have all together? The teacher will make a poster to remind you of all your ideas about what to do when you are alone and bored.

DRAWING OUT © 1992 by Prentice-Hall, Inc.
Permission granted to reproduce for classroom use.

A Gift Box for a Friend

Here is an empty gift box. Draw a present in the box to give to your best friend. What is something your friend really wants to have?

WRITE ABOUT YOUR DRAWING

What is in the gift box and who is it for? _____

_____

Share your drawing and your sentences with your classmates. Tell more about your friend and the gift you are giving.

BRAINSTORM!

Sit down in groups of four. We all love to receive presents, but sometimes we receive presents that are a little strange—presents that we don't like or can't use. With your partners, brainstorm a list of presents that you **like** to **receive** on your birthday or on a holiday.

1. _____
2. _____
3. _____
4. _____
5. _____
6. _____
7. _____
8. _____
9. _____
10. _____
11. _____
12. _____

Now, make a list of **strange** presents you have received before, or presents you **don't** think are very fun or interesting.

1. _____
2. _____
3. _____
4. _____
5. _____
6. _____
7. _____
8. _____
9. _____
10. _____
11. _____
12. _____

When you have finished, share your list with the whole class to see if your lists are similar or different.

Who Is It?

All the students will write their names on a small piece of paper and put the names in a box. Each student will pull a name out of the box. It is a secret. Draw a picture of the classmate whose name you have. Don't write his or her name on the drawing. Your classmates will guess who it is.

DRAWING OUT © 1992 by Prentice-Hall, Inc.
Permission granted to reproduce for classroom use.

WRITE ABOUT YOUR PICTURE

This person is _____.

This person has _____.

This person likes _____.

Who is it? Can you guess?

INTERVIEW!

Sit down with a partner. Ask your partner the questions and listen **carefully**. Your partner will question you the same way. *If you don't want to answer some of the questions, just say, "I pass on that question."*

When your interview is **finished,** write your partner's answers on the lines as you remember them. Begin your sentences with "she" and "her" or "he" and "his."

When the teacher says that time is up, trade papers with your partner. Read what your partner has written and correct any information that he or she may have that is not correct. Return the paper to your partner.

1. What is your full name?

   _____

2. Do you like your name? Would you like to change your name? If yes, what name would you like to have?

   _____

3. What do you like to do on the weekends?

   _____

4. What do you miss most about your native country?

   _____

   _____

5. What is something you especially like about living here in this country?

   _____

   _____

6. How much time do you spend watching TV?

   _____

7. Are you married or single? What do you like best about being married or single?

   _____

   _____

8. Are you a morning person or a night person?

   _____

9. What is something new and good in your life right now?

   _____

   _____

10. What is something you do that is good for your health?

   _____

DRAWING OUT © 1992 by Prentice-Hall, Inc.
Permission granted to reproduce for classroom use.

UNIT **2**

ALL
ABOUT
ME

Things I Like to Eat

What do you like to eat? Draw your four favorite foods here in the four spaces.

WRITE ABOUT YOUR DRAWINGS

My four favorite foods are:

1. _____   3. _____
2. _____   4. _____

Share your drawings and list of favorite foods with your classmates. Tell more about things you like to eat. Do you like American food? What kind of American food do you like? Can you cook? What can you cook?

WRITE ABOUT IT!

You are going to invite your friends over to your home for dinner on Friday evening. You want to serve them food from your country. What will you serve to them? Write your plans for your dinner.

_____

_____

_____

_____

_____

_____

_____

_____

_____

_____

_____

What is your favorite dinner dish from your country? What are the ingredients? How is it made? Write the recipe here.

_____

_____

_____

_____

_____

_____

_____

_____

_____

_____

_____

Sit down in groups of four. Tell your partners about your dinner plans and your special recipe.

DRAWING OUT © 1992 by Prentice-Hall, Inc.
Permission granted to reproduce for classroom use.

What Do You Need?

We all need things. Draw pictures of four things that you need but you do not have right now. They may be things for your house or for your family or just for you.

WRITE ABOUT YOUR DRAWINGS

I need _____.
I need _____.
I need _____.
I need _____.

Share your drawings and sentences with your classmates. Tell more about the things you need.

BRAINSTORM!

Look at this baby. She is crying. What does she need? Make a list of 15 things this baby **needs** to be happy.

1. _____
2. _____
3. _____
4. _____
5. _____
6. _____
7. _____
8. _____
9. _____
10. _____
11. _____
12. _____
13. _____
14. _____
15. _____

Look at this man. He is **very** happy. He has **everything** he needs to be happy. Make a list of 12 things this man **has** that make him happy.

1. _____
2. _____
3. _____
4. _____
5. _____
6. _____
7. _____
8. _____
9. _____
10. _____
11. _____
12. _____

What Do You Have?

You have *a lot* of things. Draw four things that you *have* and *like*—four special things, large or small.

WRITE ABOUT YOUR PICTURES

I have a _____ and I like it because _____
_____

I have a _____ and I like it because _____
_____

I have a _____ and I like it because _____
_____

I have a _____ and I like it because _____
_____

Share your drawings and sentences with your classmates. Tell more about these four things you have.

WRITE ABOUT IT!

You have **one** very special thing in your house. It belongs to you. Write about this special thing. What is it? Where did you get it? How long have you had it? Why is it so special to you?

_____

_____

_____

_____

_____

_____

_____

_____

_____

_____

_____

What is one very special thing you **wish** you had? Describe this thing. What would it look like? Why do you want it?

_____

_____

_____

_____

_____

_____

_____

_____

_____

_____

_____

_____

Sit down in groups of four. Tell your partners about the one special thing that **you have** in your house. Then tell your group about the one thing you **wish you had**.

My Usual Day

Think about Mondays. Think about Wednesdays. What do you do on a usual day? Draw pictures of three things you do on a usual day—morning, afternoon, and evening.

MORNING

AFTERNOON

EVENING

WRITE ABOUT YOUR DRAWINGS

On a usual morning, I _____.

On a usual afternoon, I _____.

On a usual evening, I _____.

Share your drawings and sentences with your classmates. Tell more about your usual day. Is your usual day very similar to your friends' usual days or is it very different?

WRITE ABOUT IT!

Was yesterday a usual day for you? Think about your day yesterday. Where were you yesterday morning? What were you doing? Who were you with? Was it a good morning or not so good? Why? Write about your morning.

_____

_____

_____

_____

_____

_____

_____

_____

_____

_____

_____

_____

Was yesterday evening a usual evening for you? Where were you? What were you doing? Who were you with? Was it a good evening or not so good? Why? Write about your evening.

_____

_____

_____

_____

_____

_____

_____

_____

_____

_____

_____

_____

_____

DRAWING OUT © 1992 by Prentice-Hall, Inc. Permission granted to reproduce for classroom use.

Bad Habits

Do you have a bad habit? Do you do something that you know is not good for you or that is not correct but you just do it anyway? Almost everyone has a bad habit. Make a picture of a bad habit you have that you would like to change.

WRITE ABOUT YOUR DRAWING

One bad habit I have is _____

_____

I would like to change this bad habit because _____

_____

Share your drawing and sentences with your classmates. Tell more about bad habits. Do any of your classmates have the same bad habit as yours? Talk about how we can change our bad habits.

BRAINSTORM!

Sit down in groups of four. You are all housemates. It is very hard to live with your housemates sometimes. Everyone has so many bad habits! Together make a list of all the bad habits your group of housemates has that must be changed if you are going to live together in peace and harmony. Look at the examples given.

1. Someone forgets to wash his dishes and leaves them in the sink.
2. Someone never pays her share of the telephone bill.
3. Someone drinks all the sodas in the refrigerator and doesn't buy any.
4. _____
5. _____
6. _____
7. _____
8. _____
9. _____
10. _____
11. _____
12. _____

When you are finished making your list, share your ideas orally with the whole class. Are your ideas different or similar? Your teacher will make a poster of all your ideas to remind you of habits we might want to change in order to get along better with our housemates!

DRAWING OUT © 1992 by Prentice-Hall, Inc.
Permission granted to reproduce for classroom use.

Taste, Sound, Smell, Look, and Feel

Draw five small pictures: **1)** something that tastes delicious, **2)** something that sounds beautiful, **3)** something that smells nice, **4)** something that looks pretty, and **5)** something that feels good.

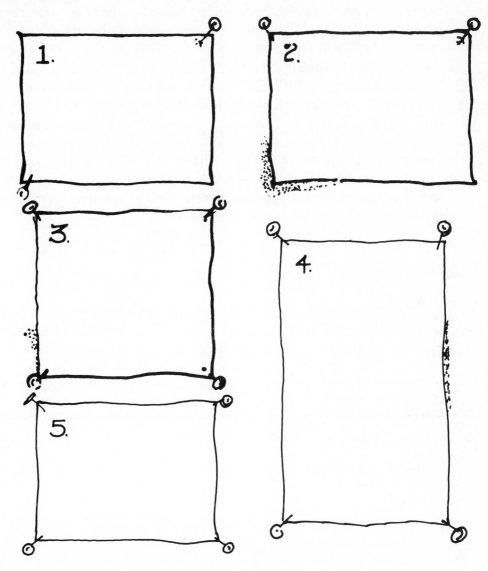

WRITE ABOUT YOUR DRAWINGS

1. Something that tastes delicious is _____.
2. Something that sounds beautiful is _____.
3. Something that smells nice is _____.
4. Something that looks pretty is _____.
5. Something that feels good is _____.

Share your drawings and sentences with your classmates. Tell more about things that look, taste, smell, feel, and sound good to you.

BRAINSTORM!

Sit down in groups of four. Decide which two of you are "city slickers" (people who were born in a big city and live in a big city now) and which two of you are "country bumpkins" (people who were born in the countryside or on a farm and still live in the country).

Talk first of all about "city life." What are all the good things about living in the city and all the not so good things about living in the city? Make a list of what you see, smell, and hear there and how you might feel. What can you **do** in the city and what are the **problems**?

Then make a list about "country life." What are all the good things about living in the country and all the not so good things about living in the country? What do you see, smell, and hear there? What can you **do** in the country and what are the **problems**?

CITY — GOOD

_____
_____
_____
_____
_____

CITY — NOT SO GOOD

_____
_____
_____
_____
_____

COUNTRY — GOOD

_____
_____
_____
_____
_____

COUNTRY — NOT SO GOOD

_____
_____
_____
_____
_____

How Do You Feel?

What makes you angry? What makes you happy? What makes you nervous? Draw pictures of things that make you happy, angry, **or** nervous.

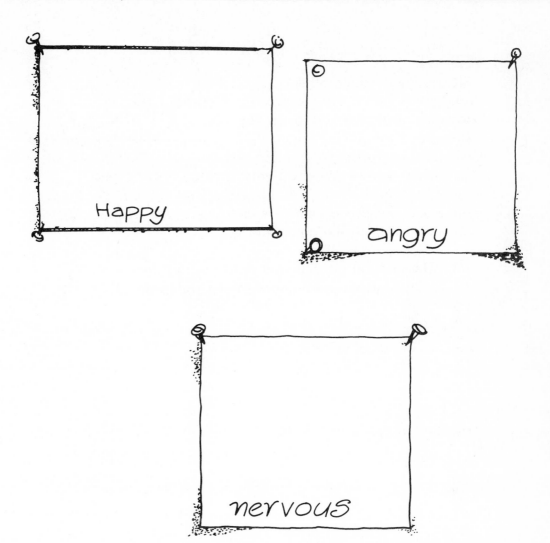

WRITE ABOUT YOUR PICTURES

_____ makes me feel _____.

_____ makes me feel _____.

_____ makes me feel _____.

Share your drawings and sentences with your classmates. Tell more about how you feel _today_ and why.

BRAINSTORM!

Sit down with three other students. Look at this picture together. This man just got a **big surprise** in the mail. It might be a **wonderful** surprise. Or it might be a **terrible** surprise. What do you think he is looking at? Talk about this with your group members and make a list of all the possibilities.

1. A letter from his daughter—she just got married!
2. A bill from the mechanic—$1,500 for fixing his car.
3. _____
4. _____
5. _____
6. _____
7. _____
8. _____
9. _____
10. _____
11. _____
12. _____
13. _____

When you are finished making your list, share your ideas orally with the whole class. Are your ideas different or similar?

What Do You Like? What Do You *Not* Like?

Draw four pictures: **1)** something you like, **2)** something you like *to do,* **3)** something you don't like, and **4)** something you don't like *to do.*

I LIKE...	I LIKE TO...
I DON'T LIKE...	I DON'T LIKE TO...

WRITE ABOUT YOUR DRAWINGS

I like _____.

I like to _____.

I don't like _____.

I don't like to _____.

Share your drawings and sentences with your classmates. Tell more about what you like and don't like.

INTERVIEW!

This page is a questionnaire or **survey** of preferences. Sit down with a partner. Ask your partner what he or she likes to eat, where he or she likes to go, and so on. Write your partner's answers on the lines. Your partner will question you the same way and write your answers. When you are finished, sit down in groups of four. Tell the other group members five things you learned about your partner. Trade papers with your partner after the group work!

I like to eat _____.

I don't like to eat _____.

I like to go _____.

I don't like to go _____.

I like to be _____.

I don't like to be _____.

I like to play _____.

I don't like to play _____.

A car I like is a _____.

A car I don't like is a _____.

The color I like is _____.

The color I don't like is _____.

I like to read _____.

I don't like to read _____.

I like to wear _____.

I don't like to wear _____.

An actor/actress I like is _____.

An actor/actress I don't like is _____.

The work around the house that I like is _____.

The work around the house that I don't like is _____.

A TV show I like to watch is _____.

A TV show I don't like to watch is _____.

A sport I like to watch is _____.

A sport I don't like to watch is _____.

What Can You Do?

We are *all* teachers. We can teach others many things. Can you ride a horse? Can you swim? Can you fix a broken bicycle? Can you sew? Draw pictures of **two** things that you can do and that you can teach others.

WRITE ABOUT YOUR DRAWINGS

I can teach others how to _____.

I can teach others how to _____.

Share your sentences and drawings with your classmates. Tell more about things you can do and can teach to others.

WRITE ABOUT IT!

We all have many **talents**. Some of us can draw or sing or play a musical instrument. Some of us are good dancers or athletes. Some of us like to write poems or stories. Write about one talent you **have**, and one talent you **wish** you had.

_____

_____

_____

_____

_____

_____

_____

_____

_____

_____

_____

We all have many skills. Some of us know how to type or use a computer. Some of us can repair a car or a stove. Some of us can build a house or make chocolate cookies or sew a shirt. Write about one skill that you **have** and one skill you would like to **learn**.

_____

_____

_____

_____

_____

_____

_____

_____

_____

_____

_____

DRAWING OUT © 1992 by Prentice-Hall, Inc.
Permission granted to reproduce for classroom use.

UNIT **3**

THEN AND NOW

Two Years Ago

Where were you two years ago? Were you living in a different country or city? Were you living in a different house? Were you going to school? Were you working? Make a picture about where you were two years ago and what you were doing.

WRITE ABOUT YOUR DRAWING

Two years ago I was _____

_____

_____

_____

_____

Share your drawing and your sentences with your classmates.

INTERVIEW!

Sit down with one partner. Ask your partner the questions below and listen carefully to the answers. Take notes about your partner's answers on your paper. When your interview is finished, thank your partner. Then your partner will interview you and take notes.

If you or your partner do not want to answer some of the questions, it is okay to say, "I pass on that question."

When both interviews are finished, read through your notes again and ask your partner for any missing information if it is necessary.

1. What country were you living in two years ago?
   _____

2. Were you living in the city or the country?
   _____

3. Were you working or going to school?
   _____

4. Were you living alone, with friends, or with your family?
   _____

5. What did you like about the place you were living?
   _____
   _____

6. What didn't you like about the place you were living?
   _____
   _____

7. Would you rather live there or here? Why?
   _____
   _____

When you are finished, sit down in groups of six. Tell your group members four things you learned about your partner. Be sure to trade papers when you are finished.

DRAWING OUT © 1992 by Prentice-Hall, Inc.
Permission granted to reproduce for classroom use.

Someone I Will Never Forget

We all have someone in our life that we will never forget. Who is an important person in *your* life that you will always remember? Draw a picture of that person. Write his or her name under the picture.

WRITE ABOUT YOUR DRAWING

I person I will never forget is _____ because

_____

_____

_____

Share your drawing and sentences with your classmates. Tell more about this person you will never forget.

WRITE ABOUT IT!

You have drawn a picture of a person you will never forget and told your classmates about that wonderful person. Now remember two other things and write a little paragraph about each one.

PARAGRAPH 1

Think about **a place** you visited once. A place that was special for some reason. Write about that special place. Where was it? When did you go there? What did you do there? Was anyone with you? How long did you stay there? Did you go there many times or just once? Why were you there? Why is this place a special memory?

_____

_____

_____

_____

_____

_____

_____

_____

_____

PARAGRAPH 2

Think about a special **date** in your life. (A date like June 4, 1986, or May 27, 1948, or October 21, 1989.) Write about that date. What was special about it? What happened? Where were you? Who were you with? What did you do? How did you feel?

_____

_____

_____

_____

_____

_____

_____

_____

When you are finished writing, sit down in groups of four. Take turns reading your stories to each other. Ask questions of each other about them.

DRAWING OUT © 1992 by Prentice-Hall, Inc.
Permission granted to reproduce for classroom use.

No Television

Do you watch TV a lot? Many people do. If you didn't have a television, what would you do? Draw pictures about how you would pass your time every day if you didn't have a TV.

WRITE ABOUT YOUR DRAWING

If I didn't have a TV, I would _____

_____

_____

_____

Share your drawings and sentences with your classmates. Tell more about what you would do if you didn't have a TV.

BRAINSTORM!

Sit down in groups of four. You are a *family*. Your TV has exploded. It can not be fixed. You have decided not to buy a new TV because you spend too much time sitting in front of it. You want to entertain yourselves and learn the news in other ways. With your "family," make a list together of all the other things you can do for entertainment **for free** or for **very little money**. When all groups are finished, compare your lists with the whole class.

We can find entertainment **outside our home** for very little money in the following ways:

1. Walking.
2. Going to the park.
3. _____
4. _____
5. _____
6. _____
7. _____
8. _____
9. _____
10. _____

We can entertain ourselves **in our home** by:

1. Reading a magazine.
2. Listening to music on the stereo.
3. _____
4. _____
5. _____
6. _____
7. _____
8. _____
9. _____
10. _____

DRAWING OUT © 1992 by Prentice-Hall, Inc.
Permission granted to reproduce for classroom use.

My House in My Country

Draw a picture of the house in which you used to live in your country.

☆☆☆☆☆☆☆☆☆☆☆☆☆☆☆☆☆☆☆☆☆☆☆☆☆☆☆☆☆☆☆☆☆☆
☆   ☆
☆☆☆☆☆☆☆☆☆☆☆☆☆☆☆☆☆☆☆☆☆☆☆☆☆☆☆☆☆☆☆☆☆☆

WRITE ABOUT YOUR DRAWING

What color was your house? Was it large or small? How many rooms did it have? Was it in the country or the city? What did you like best about your house in your country?

_____

_____

_____

_____

_____

Share your drawing and your sentences with your classmates. Tell more about your house and your old neighborhood.

WRITE ABOUT IT!

Sit down with a partner. Talk about what you both think would be a perfect house to live in. How big would it be? How many rooms? One or two stories? What would it have in it that is special? Where would it be—in the mountains, next to the ocean, in the city, or in the country?

Take pencils (not pens) and rulers and work together for 15 minutes to design the floor plan of this "dream home." When you have finished your house plan, write some sentences describing your dream home.

OUR DREAM HOME

_____

_____

_____

_____

_____

_____

Superstitions

A superstition is something that people believe will bring them good or bad luck. A superstition is an idea or belief that is *not* true, but that people have believed for many years in the past. For example, many people believe that it is bad luck to do business on a Friday. Some people believe that a broken mirror or a black cat brings bad luck. Draw a picture of a superstition that people from your country have or used to have.

WRITE ABOUT YOUR PICTURE

A superstition from my country: _____

_____

_____

_____

_____

Share your drawing and your sentences with your classmates. Tell more about superstitions from your country.

WRITE ABOUT IT!

Sit down with a partner. You know that a superstition is something that people believe will bring them good luck or bad luck. Superstitions are **old beliefs** that are not true. With your partner, invent and write down four **new** superstitions and decide what kind of good or bad luck they will bring.

NEW SUPERSTITION 1

You will have bad luck if _____
_____
_____ .

NEW SUPERSTITION 2

You will have bad luck if you _____
and if _____
_____ .

NEW SUPERSTITION 3

You will have good luck if _____
_____
_____ .

NEW SUPERSTITION 4

You will have good luck if you _____
and if _____
_____ .

When you have finished writing your superstitions, share them orally with the whole class or with small groups of classmates.

DRAWING OUT © 1992 by Prentice-Hall, Inc.
Permission granted to reproduce for classroom use.

Work, Work, Work!

What was your work in your country? What is your work now? What kind of work would you like to have? Draw pictures of three different jobs— your work **before**, your work **now**, and the work you **want** to have.

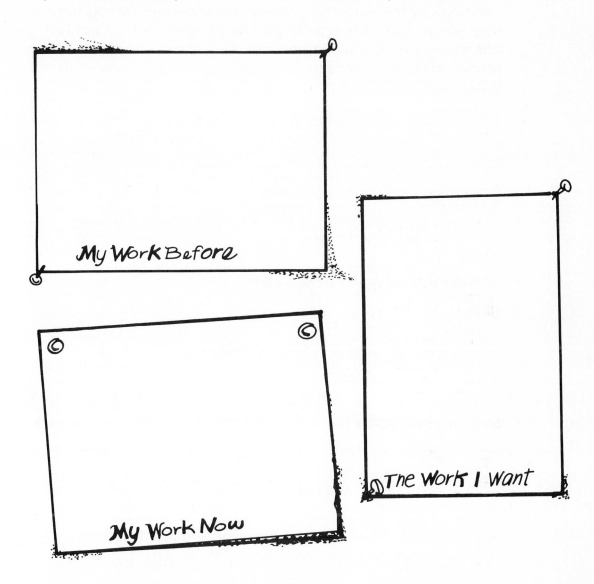

My Work Before

The Work I Want

My Work Now

WRITE ABOUT YOUR DRAWINGS

In my country, I worked as a _____.

Now, I work as a _____.

I want to work as a _____.

Share your drawings and sentences with your classmates. Tell more about your work before and your work now.

INTERVIEW!

Sit down with a partner. Ask your partner the questions and listen carefully. Write your partner's answers on the lines. Your partner will question you the same way and write your answers. If you forget what your partner said, it is okay to ask again! When you are finished, sit down in groups of four. Tell the other group members four things you learned about your partner. Trade papers with your partner after the group work.

1. What was your work in your native country?

   _____

   _____

2. How long did you do that work?

   _____

3. Did you like your work?

   _____

4. What was good about the work?

   _____

   _____

5. What was not so good about the work?

   _____

   _____

6. Have you found work in this country? If yes, what is your work?

   _____

   _____

7. Does this job pay more or less than your work in your native country?

   _____

8. Do you like the work or do you want to find other work?

   _____

   _____

9. If you could choose any work you wanted, what would you choose?

   _____

   _____

Yesterday

What day of the week was yesterday? What were you doing yesterday morning at 9:00 A.M.? What were you doing around 1:00 P.M.? What were you doing around 7:00 P.M. yesterday? Draw three pictures about what you were doing yesterday.

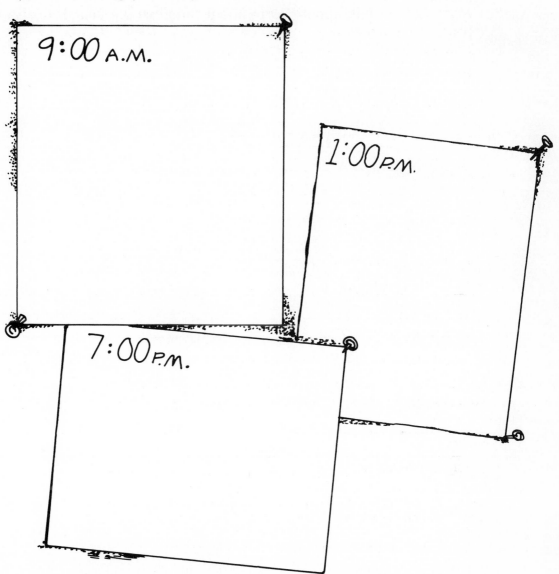

WRITE ABOUT YOUR DRAWINGS

Yesterday morning about 9:00 A.M. I was _____.

Yesterday afternoon about 1:00 P.M. I was _____.

Yesterday evening about 7:00 P.M. I was _____.

Share your drawings and sentences with your classmates. Tell more about yesterday.

WRITE ABOUT IT!

Did you see or talk to anyone yesterday? A friend? A neighbor? Someone on the street or in class or on a bus? Think about the people who passed through your life yesterday. Who were they? Where did you see them? What did you talk about? Write about three people you saw or spoke to yesterday.

1. _____
_____
_____
_____
_____
_____
_____
_____

2. _____
_____
_____
_____
_____
_____
_____
_____

3. _____
_____
_____
_____
_____
_____
_____
_____

When you are finished writing, sit down with one partner. Tell your partner about the people you saw and spoke with yesterday.

DRAWING OUT © 1992 by Prentice-Hall, Inc.
Permission granted to reproduce for classroom use.

A Happy Day

We all can remember very happy days. Can you remember one happy day in your life? Maybe a long time ago, or maybe just a week ago? Where were you? Who were you with? What were you doing? Draw a picture of the happy day you remember.

WRITE ABOUT YOUR DRAWING

I remember one happy day when I was _____

_____

_____

_____

_____

_____

Share your drawing and sentences with your classmates.

INTERVIEW!

Sit down with a partner. Ask your partner the questions and listen carefully. Write your partner's answers on the lines. Your partner will question you the same way and write your answers. If you forget what your partner said, it is okay to ask again! When you are finished, sit down in groups of four. Tell the other group members what you learned about your partner. Trade papers with your partner after the group work.

Tell me about one happy day you remember.

1. When was the happy day?

_____

_____

2. Where were you?

_____

_____

3. What were you doing?

_____

_____

4. Who were you with?

_____

_____

5. Why was it an especially happy day?

_____

_____

Five Good Minutes

Think about your day yesterday. Your day was 24 hours long. Did you have *five good minutes* yesterday? Which five minutes did you like best? Draw a picture of five good minutes you had yesterday.

WRITE ABOUT YOUR DRAWING

I had five good minutes yesterday when _____

_____

_____

_____

_____.

Share your drawing and your sentences with your classmates. Tell more about your five good minutes.

BRAINSTORM!

You have told your friends about your five good minutes yesterday. You have listened to your friends telling about their five good minutes. Think about the kinds of things that cause us to have bad days or good days. Make a list of ten things that go wrong that cause us to have a bad day. Make a list of things that add up to a good day. Look at the examples. When you are finished writing, sit down in groups of six to share your lists. Are they the same or different?

A **bad** day is when. . .

1. You lose your keys.
2. You break a cup.
3. Your children are sick.
4. _____
5. _____
6. _____
7. _____
8. _____
9. _____
10. _____

A **good** day is when. . .

1. You find $10 in your pocket.
2. A friend invites you to lunch.
3. You can sleep until 10:00 A.M.
4. _____
5. _____
6. _____
7. _____
8. _____
9. _____
10. _____

PEOPLE
AND
CONVERSATIONS

Who Are These People?

Draw two people on this page—one man and one woman. They can be young or old and any nationality you like.

WRITE ABOUT YOUR DRAWINGS

1. His name is _____. He is _____ years old. He works as a _____ and he likes _____. Every day he _____.

2. Her name is _____. She is _____ years old. She works as a _____ and she likes _____. Every day she _____.

Share your drawings and sentences with your classmates. Tell more about these people.

WRITE ABOUT IT!

Sit down with a partner. Look at this
picture together. This man is 80 years old.
With your partner, write a poem about this
man. Take turns finishing the sentences.
Read carefully what your partner writes, so
that you can continue the writing as one
complete poem. (It is not necessary to
rhyme the lines!)

HE IS AN OLD MAN.

HE LIKES _____

HE HAS _____

EVERY DAY HE _____

AND _____

HE IS AN OLD MAN.

HE WAS _____

BUT NOW HE IS _____

HE USED TO _____

BUT NOW _____

ALL HE REALLY WANTS IS _____

HE IS AN OLD MAN.

When you have finished your poem, sit down in groups of six. Share your
poems orally with each other. Then the teacher may ask for five
volunteers to come to the front of the class to read for the whole group.

Americans: A Conversation

Do you know many Americans? Do they talk to you? Do you have conversations with them? Draw the faces of three Americans. Draw your face.

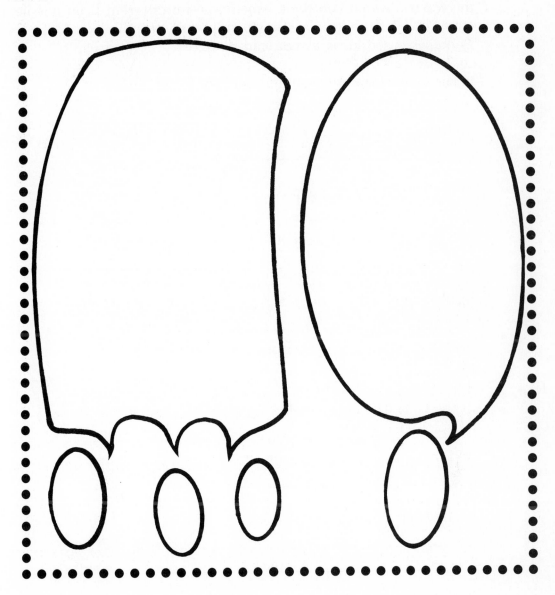

WRITE ABOUT YOUR DRAWING

What do Americans say to you? What do you say to them? In the balloons, write a conversation between you and the Americans.

Share your drawing and writing with your classmates. Tell more about the kinds of conversations you have with Americans.

BRAINSTORM!

Sit down in groups of four. Americans! Are they very different from people in your country? Or are they the same? Discuss with your group the ways in which you think Americans are different from people in your countries. Talk about ways in which people are all alike. Make a list with as many shared ideas as you can think of.

In the United States, people. . .

_____

And in _____ people. . .

_____

In the United States, people. . .

_____

And in _____ people. . .

_____

In the United States, people. . .

_____

And in _____ people. . .

_____

In the United States, people. . .

_____

And in _____ people. . .

_____

In the United States, people. . .

_____

And in _____ people. . .

_____

In the United States, people. . .

_____

And in _____ people. . .

_____

When you are finished with your list, share your ideas orally with the whole class. How many ideas does the class have all together?

DRAWING OUT © 1992 by Prentice-Hall, Inc.
Permission granted to reproduce for classroom use.

Your Teacher

Look at your teacher very carefully. Draw a picture of him or her.

WRITE ABOUT YOUR DRAWING

Our teacher is _____.

Our teacher feels _____ today.

Everyday he/she _____.

Something our teacher always says to us is "_____

_____."

Our teacher likes _____.

Share your drawing and sentences with your classmates. Tell more about your teacher.

WRITE ABOUT IT!

Throughout our life many people—our schoolteachers, our parents, our grandparents, our neighbors, and our friends—teach us many important things.

Think about someone who was a good teacher for you at one time in your life. Describe this person. Say where and when you knew this person. Tell something that this person taught you.

SOMEONE WHO TAUGHT ME SOMETHING IMPORTANT

_____

_____

_____

_____

_____

_____

_____

_____

_____

_____

_____

_____

_____

_____

_____

_____

When you have finished writing about your good "teacher," sit down in groups of four and share your stories with each other.

On the Bus: A Conversation

You are on the bus alone. A classmate gets on the bus and sees you. Work with a partner. On this paper, draw yourself. Your partner will draw himself or herself.

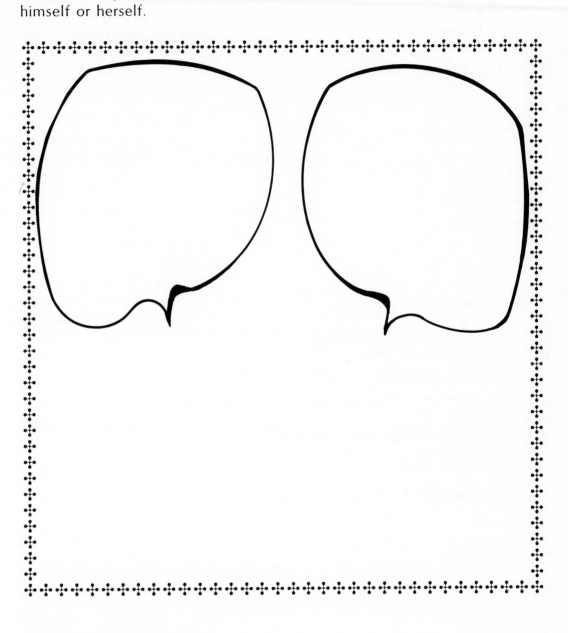

WRITE A CONVERSATION

You are both on the bus. You met by accident. In the balloons, write a conversation between you and your friend.

Share your drawings and conversations with other classmates.

INTERVIEW!

Sit down with a partner. Ask your partner the questions. Listen **carefully**. Your partner will question you the same way. When both interviews are finished, thank your partner, read the questions again silently, and write answers according to your own thoughts.

1. Do you ever ride the bus in this city? If yes, where do you go on the bus?

   _____

   _____

2. What do you think of the cost of riding the bus? What do you think of the bus service in this city?

   _____

   _____

3. Do you have a car? If yes, what kind of car do you drive?

   _____

   _____

4. Did you have a car in your native country? If yes, what kind of car was it?

   _____

   _____

5. Have you ever traveled on a train? If yes, where and when have you traveled on a train? Do you like train travel? What do you like about trains?

   _____

   _____

   _____

6. Have you ever traveled on an airplane? If yes, where and when did you fly? Do you like flying?

   _____

   _____

   _____

7. Would you like to go up in a hot-air balloon? Would it be fun or scary?

   _____

   _____

8. Have you ever traveled on a boat or a ship? If yes, what did you think of water travel? When and where did you travel by boat or ship?

   _____

   _____

   _____

DRAWING OUT © 1992 by Prentice-Hall, Inc.
Permission granted to reproduce for classroom use.

Who Helps You?

In the United States, do you need help sometimes? Who offers you some help? Draw a picture of a person who helps you sometimes.

WRITE ABOUT YOUR DRAWING

A person in the United States who helps me is _____.

Sometimes I need help when _____

_____

_____

_____

Share your picture and sentences with your classmates. Tell more about this person who helps you. What kind of person is he or she? Where did you meet him or her?

BRAINSTORM!

Sit down with one partner. Newcomer students or immigrants to the United States need to learn English, but they also need to learn about the **way of life** or the way of doing things in the United States. We ask ourselves all the time, "How do they do this here? How does this machine work? Where can I find a . . . ? What are the rules about . . . ? What am I supposed to do first? Where must I go to . . . ?" and so on.

As an immigrant or foreign student in the United States, what were or are some of the things you have trouble with? What are some things that are very different here and that you needed help with in order to feel more sure of yourself and comfortable here? Discuss this with your partner and make a list together of some of the problem areas for newcomers.

1. _____

_____

2. _____

_____

3. _____

_____

4. _____

_____

5. _____

_____

6. _____

_____

7. _____

_____

8. _____

_____

9. _____

_____

10. _____

_____

When you have completed your list, share your ideas orally with the whole class. How many of you have experienced the same thing?

The Doctor's Office: A Conversation

You are sitting in the waiting room of the doctor's office. Your classmate comes in to see the doctor, too. Work with a partner on this piece of paper. You draw yourself. Your partner will draw himself or herself.

WRITE A CONVERSATION

In the balloons, write a conversation between you and your classmate in the doctor's office.

Share your drawings and conversations with other classmates.

BRAINSTORM!

Sit down in groups of four. No one wants to be sick. No one wants to have accidents. No one likes to have to go to the doctor. We can't always avoid visits to the doctor's office, but we can do something to prevent medical problems. For example, we can watch our diet and we can do activities that are good for the body. With your partners, discuss and write down foods we can eat that are healthful and foods that we should stay away from. Discuss and write down activities that are dangerous to your health and those that help to keep you healthy. Make four short lists.

HEALTHFUL FOODS

1. spinach

2. _____

3. _____

4. _____

5. _____

6. _____

FOODS TO AVOID

1. fat meat

2. _____

3. _____

4. _____

5. _____

6. _____

HEALTHFUL ACTIVITIES

1. swimming

2. _____

3. _____

4. _____

5. _____

6. _____

ACTIVITIES TO AVOID

1. smoking

2. _____

3. _____

4. _____

5. _____

6. _____

When you have finished your list, share it orally with the whole class. Are your ideas different or similar? Your teacher will make a poster of all your ideas to remind you of ways to stay healthy.

Break Time: A Conversation

It is break time at school. You are drinking coffee. A classmate is drinking coffee, too. Work with a partner. On this paper, draw yourself. Your partner will draw himself or herself.

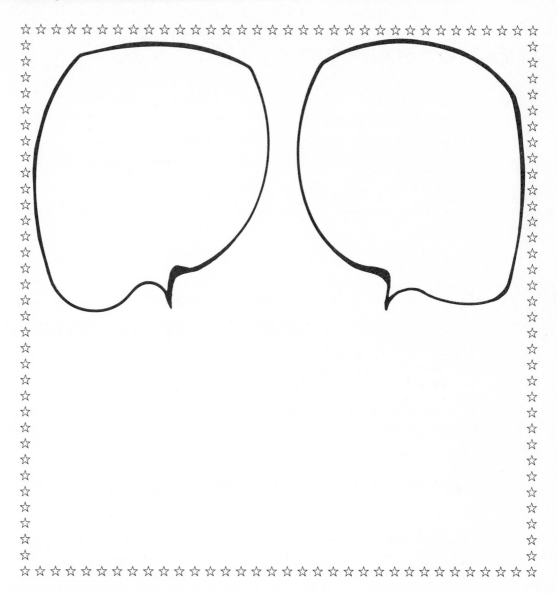

WRITE A CONVERSATION

You are both drinking coffee at break time. In the balloons, write a conversation between you and your classmate.

Share your drawings and conversation with other classmates.

BRAINSTORM!

Sit down in groups of four. Break times at school give you the opportunity to meet with your friends and classmates and practice your English conversation. There are many things you can do to learn English quickly in addition to going to classes and studying your text books. With your partners, brainstorm a list of 16 different things you can do to help yourself learn English quickly.

1. _____
2. _____
3. _____
4. _____
5. _____
6. _____
7. _____
8. _____
9. _____
10. _____
11. _____
12. _____
13. _____
14. _____
15. _____
16. _____

When you have finished your list, share it orally with the whole class. The teacher will make a poster of all your ideas to remind you of learning opportunities.

A Gift Box for a Classmate

Write your name on a small piece of paper. The teacher will collect all the students' names and put them in a box. Pull a name out of the box and think of a present you will give to the student whose name you have. Draw the present for your classmate in the gift box.

TO: _____

FROM: _____

When everyone is ready, stand up and give your present to your classmate. When you sit down again, tell your classmates what present you received and who gave it to you.

BRAINSTORM!

Sit down in groups of four. We all love to receive and give presents. People in the United States give presents on birthdays, in December at Christmas time, and on other special occasions. Make a list together of special occasions or dates when people give presents in **your** country. Give an example of the **kind** of gift that is usually given on those special days.

SPECIAL DAY OR OCCASION	EXAMPLE OF GIFT
1. _____	_____
2. _____	_____
3. _____	_____
4. _____	_____
5. _____	_____
6. _____	_____
7. _____	_____
8. _____	_____
9. _____	_____
10. _____	_____
11. _____	_____
12. _____	_____
13. _____	_____
14. _____	_____

When you have finished your list, share it orally with the whole class. Are your ideas similar or different?

At a Dance: A Conversation

You are at a dance alone. Your classmate comes to the dance alone, too. Work with a partner. On this paper, draw yourself. Your partner will draw himself or herself.

WRITE A CONVERSATION

You are both at the dance. You met there by accident. In the balloons, write a conversation between you and your classmate.

Share your drawing and conversation with other classmates.

BRAINSTORM!

Sit down in groups of four. When you have moved to a new city or country, and you are trying to speak and understand English better, it is often difficult to meet new people and to build a "social life." Even when you have lived in a town for a long time and your English is *perfect,* it is sometimes not easy to make friends! How do you make friends in the city you live in now? Where do you go? What do you do? With your group members, discuss possible places to go or things to do to find new friends. Make a list.

1. _____
2. _____
3. _____
4. _____
5. _____
6. _____
7. _____
8. _____
9. _____
10. _____
11. _____
12. _____
13. _____
14. _____

When you have finished your list, share it orally with the whole class. Are your ideas similar or different? Your teacher will make a poster of all your ideas to remind you of opportunities to make new friends.

*DREAMS
AND
PLANS*

The Perfect Husband

What kind of a man is the perfect husband? Draw a perfect husband on this paper.

WRITE ABOUT YOUR DRAWING

The perfect husband is:

_____ _____ _____

_____ _____ _____

Share your drawing and writing with a group of five classmates. Do you all agree on what makes a perfect husband? Are your ideas very different?

BRAINSTORM!

Sit down in groups of four. You have drawn a picture of the perfect husband. But no one is perfect, unfortunately. Real husbands have faults—or qualities that are hard to live with. They also have good qualities—qualities that make you glad that they are your husbands. You have to take the good with the bad!

With your partners, brainstorm two lists. One list is all the good or positive qualities that a woman looks for in a husband. The other list is for all the faults or negative qualities that are hard to live with.

POSITIVE QUALITIES	NEGATIVE QUALITIES
1. He likes his work.	**1.** He stays out too much at night.
2. He is romantic.	**2.** He drinks too much beer.
3. _____	**3.** _____
4. _____	**4.** _____
5. _____	**5.** _____
6. _____	**6.** _____
7. _____	**7.** _____
8. _____	**8.** _____
9. _____	**9.** _____
10. _____	**10.** _____
11. _____	**11.** _____

Is it possible to change your husband's negative qualities? Discuss this question with your group.

When you have finished your lists, the teacher will ask some groups to share them with the whole class to check for similarities and differences.

DRAWING OUT © 1992 by Prentice-Hall, Inc.
Permission granted to reproduce for classroom use.

The Perfect Wife

What kind of woman is the perfect wife? Draw the perfect wife on this paper.

WRITE ABOUT YOUR DRAWING

The perfect wife is:

_____ _____ _____

_____ _____ _____

Share your drawing and writing with a group of five classmates. Do you all agree on what makes a perfect wife? Are your ideas very different?

BRAINSTORM!

Sit down in groups of four. Look at the list below. These are positive qualities that men look for in a wife. **Work alone** for three minutes. Write a number 1 on the line next to what you think is the most important quality for a wife to have. Write a number 2 next to the second most important quality. Choose only eight qualities and mark them from 1 to 8 according to importance.

POSITIVE QUALITIES FOR A WIFE TO HAVE

____ She is a good cook.

____ She is very intelligent and has a good education.

____ She loves children and wants many of them.

____ She is very sexy and romantic.

____ She makes me laugh; she is a happy person.

____ She is a very good housekeeper.

____ She has a lot of money and is generous.

____ She is beautiful.

____ She is young.

____ She is very talented.

____ She has a good job.

____ She is a good listener.

____ She is religious.

____ She is in excellent health.

____ (other?) _____

When your three minutes are up, share your top five choices with your group. Write down on a separate piece of paper those qualities **most** of you agree on. Your teacher will call on some groups to share their top five choices with the whole class and write them on the board.

Dreams

You are in your bed. You are asleep. What are you dreaming about?
Draw your face. Draw a picture of your dream.

WRITE ABOUT YOUR DRAWING

I am sleeping and I am dreaming about _____

_____

_____

_____

Share your drawing and sentences with your classmates. Tell more about
your dream.

INTERVIEW!

Sit down with a partner. Ask your partner the questions and listen carefully. Write your partner's answers on the lines. Your partner will question you the same way and write your answers. If you forget what your partner said, it is okay to ask again! When you are finished, sit down in groups of four. Tell the other group members four things you learned about your partner. Trade papers with your partner after the group work.

1. Do you sometimes remember your dreams when you wake up?

   _____

2. Do you dream in color?

   _____

3. Do you ever dream that you are speaking English? If yes, who do you talk to in your dream? Is your English good or bad in your dreams?

   _____
   _____
   _____
   _____

4. Have you ever dreamed the same dream more than once? If yes, what is the dream about?

   _____
   _____
   _____
   _____

5. What is your idea of a good dream?

   _____
   _____
   _____

6. Do you ever have nightmares (bad dreams)? If yes, what is an example of a nightmare you have had?

   _____
   _____
   _____
   _____
   _____

The Lottery

You have won the lottery for $1 million. What will you do with this money? Draw pictures about how you will spend your lottery money.

WRITE ABOUT YOUR DRAWING

I will spend my lottery money on _____

_____

_____

_____

_____

Share your drawing and sentences with your classmates. Tell more about how you will spend your lottery prize.

INTERVIEW!

Sit down with a partner. Ask your partner the questions and listen carefully. Write your partner's answers on the lines. Your partner will question you the same way and write your answers. If you forget what your partner said, it is okay to ask again! When you are finished, sit down in groups of four. Tell the other group members four things you learned about your partner. Trade papers with your partner after the group work.

1. Have you ever bought a lottery ticket? If **not**, why not? Give three reasons.

   _____

   _____

   _____

2. How often do you buy lottery tickets?

   _____

3. Have you ever won any money playing the lottery?

   _____

4. Is there a national lottery in your native country?

   _____

5. What is **good** about a national lottery?

   _____

   _____

6. What is **not so good** about a national lottery?

   _____

   _____

7. Do you know anyone personally who has won a lot of money in the lottery?

   _____

8. Do other people in your family play the lottery?

   _____

9. Where is a good place to buy lottery tickets in this town?

   _____

DRAWING OUT © 1992 by Prentice-Hall, Inc. Permission granted to reproduce for classroom use.

Five Years from Today

Where do you want to be five years from today? What do you want to be doing? Who do you want to be with? Draw a picture about where you want to be five years from today.

WRITE ABOUT YOUR DRAWING

Where do you want to be, with whom, and doing what?

_____

_____

_____

_____

_____

Share your drawing and sentences with your classmates.

INTERVIEW!

Sit down with a partner. Ask your partner the questions and listen carefully. Write your partner's answers on the lines. Your partner will question you the same way and write your answers. If you forget what your partner said, it is okay to ask again! When you are finished, sit down in groups of four. Tell the other group members what you learned about your partner. Trade papers with your partner after the group work.

1. Where do you want to be five years from today?

_____

_____

_____

_____

_____

2. What do you want to be doing?

_____

_____

_____

_____

_____

3. Do you want to be working or going to school? If so, where?

_____

_____

_____

_____

_____

4. Are you making any special plans to help you achieve this goal?

_____

_____

_____

_____

This Weekend

What are you going to do this coming weekend? How will you spend Saturday? What are you going to do on Sunday? Draw two pictures about what you will do this weekend.

WRITE ABOUT YOUR DRAWING

On Saturday, I am going to _____

_____

_____.

On Sunday, I am going to _____

_____

_____.

Share your drawings and sentences with your classmates. Tell more about your weekend plans.

WRITE ABOUT IT!

What do you enjoy doing on the weekend or on your days off from work? What do you like **to do for fun**?

What kind of **work do you have to do** on the weekend or on your days off from work? Are you busy around the house?

On the weekends or when I am not working, I **like to** . . .

1. _____
2. _____
3. _____
4. _____
5. _____

On the weekends or when I am not working, I **have to do things around the house,** such as . . .

1. _____
2. _____
3. _____
4. _____
5. _____

When you have finished writing, sit down with one partner. Compare your ideas. Are they similar or different? The teacher may ask some volunteers to read their papers to the whole class for comparison.

Five Hundred Dollars

You have $500 and you can spend it only on yourself. You are going to buy something very special that you have wanted for a long time. Draw a picture of what you are going to buy.

WRITE ABOUT YOUR DRAWING

What are you going to buy? What will it look like? Where are you going to buy it? Why do you want to buy this thing?

_____

_____

_____

_____

Share your drawings and sentences with your classmates. Tell more about the thing you are going to buy.

WRITE ABOUT IT!

You have $1 million. You are going to give it all to people who need it—to three different charities. Which charities will you give it to? Why?

1. _____
_____
_____
_____
_____

2. _____
_____
_____
_____
_____

3. _____
_____
_____
_____
_____

When you have finished writing, sit down with one partner. Compare your ideas. Are they similar or different? The teacher may ask some volunteers to read their papers to the whole class for comparison.

Someday

What will you do in the future . . . someday? Draw a picture of something you will *learn,* something you will *see,* some place you will *go,* **or** something you will *have.*

WRITE ABOUT YOUR DRAWING

Someday I will _____

_____

_____

_____

_____

_____.

Share your drawing and sentences with your classmates. Tell more about what you will do someday.

DRAWING OUT © 1992 by Prentice-Hall, Inc.
Permission granted to reproduce for classroom use.

97

WRITE ABOUT IT!

We all have dreams about our future. What are your dreams or fantasies about "someday"? If you could **be** or **do** or **have** anything or **go** anywhere, what would happen for you?

_____

_____

_____

_____

_____

_____

_____

_____

_____

_____

Do you think this will **really** happen for you? Why? Why not? What must happen or change before this dream could come true?

_____

_____

_____

_____

_____

_____

_____

_____

_____

When you have finished writing, sit down with one partner. Compare your ideas. Are they similar or different? The teacher may ask some volunteers to read their papers to the whole class for comparison.

A Very Special Day

Today is a very special day. It is **not** a usual day. It is a **perfect** day for you. You can do anything you like. You have $100 and you have a car with a full gas tank. Draw a picture about what you will do on your very special day.

WRITE ABOUT YOUR DRAWING

Where will you go? Who will you see? What will you do?

_____

_____

_____

_____

_____

Share your drawing and sentences with your classmates. Tell more about your very special day.

INTERVIEW!

Sit down with one partner. On a small piece of paper, draw a $1,000 bill. Give your partner the $1,000 for vacation money. Ask your partner the questions below and listen carefully to the answers. Take notes on your paper. When your interview is finished, your partner will give you $1,000 for your vacation and ask you the questions.

When both interviews are finished, sit down in groups of four. Tell the group what you learned about your partner's vacation plans. Trade papers with your partner after talking to the group.

Here is $1,000. It is money for your vacation.

1. Where will you go for your vacation?

_____

_____

2. Why will you go there?

_____

_____

3. Will you take anyone with you? Or will you meet someone special there? If yes, who?

_____

_____

4. What will you do there?

_____

_____

5. How long will you stay?

_____

_____

DRAWING OUT © 1992 by Prentice-Hall, Inc.
Permission granted to reproduce for classroom use.

UNIT **6**

FANTASIES AND INVENTIONS

What Are They Carrying?

Draw a big box in the man's hands. Draw a basket on the woman's arm. Draw a large bag in the boy's hand.

WRITE ABOUT YOUR DRAWING

What is in the box? Where is the man going? _____

_____

_____

What is in the basket? Where is the woman going? _____

_____

_____

What is in the large bag? Where is the boy going? _____

_____

_____

Share your drawings and sentences with your classmates. Tell more about these people.

WRITE ABOUT IT!

Finish this story:

I came home from school yesterday about an hour after class. I unlocked the door. No one was at home. I walked into the kitchen, opened the refrigerator, and took out a soda. As I opened the soda can, I turned around and saw a box on the table. It was wrapped like a present. I walked over to the box and saw that my name was on the tag. It was signed, "To a very special person with love." But it wasn't my birthday. I had no idea what was in the box or who it was from or how it got on my table. I slowly took off the wrapping paper and opened the box. Inside the box was the most wonderful present I could ever receive—something I really wanted and needed right now but never expected to have. I didn't know who gave it to me. I could only guess . . .

_____

_____

_____

_____

_____

_____

_____

_____

_____

_____

_____

_____

_____

_____

_____

_____

_____

_____

_____

When you have finished writing, sit down in groups of four. Share your story ending orally with your partners. As a group, decide which story ending you like best. The teacher will ask for volunteers to share the "best" endings with the whole class.

A Flag

You are the president of a new country. You need a flag. Draw a flag for your new country. Put *three symbols* on your flag that tell us about what is important to you as president of this new country.

WRITE ABOUT YOUR DRAWING

What does your new flag look like? What do the symbols mean?

_____

_____

_____

_____

Share your flag and writing with your classmates. Tell more about what is important to you as president of this new country.

WRITE ABOUT IT!

Think about the flag of your native country. What colors are on it? What designs or symbols are on it? What do the designs or symbols mean?

Describe your country's flag.

_____

_____

_____

_____

When you see your country's flag, what does it make you think about?

_____

_____

_____

_____

Describe the American flag.

_____

_____

_____

_____

When you see the American flag, what do you think of?

_____

_____

_____

_____

When you have finished your writing, sit down in groups of four. Share your ideas orally with your partners. The teacher will ask each student to share their answer to the last question—"What do you think of when you see the American flag?"—with the whole class.

The Unfinished Picture

Look at the drawing. It is not finished. What does it look like to you? Add some more lines and details to this picture so that we can see what it is. You may turn it sideways or upside down if you like!

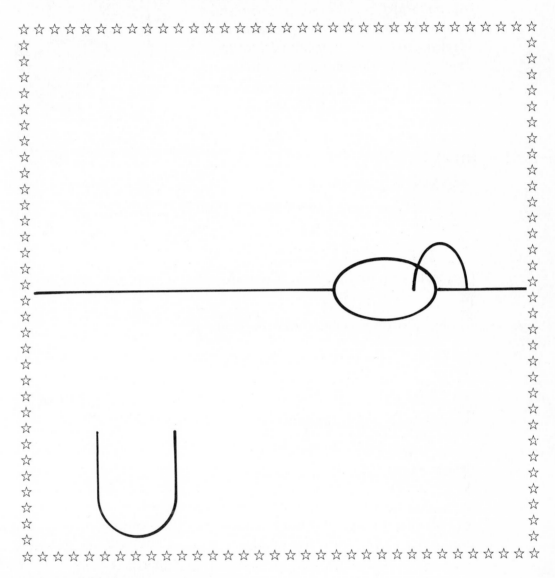

WRITE ABOUT YOUR PICTURE

Give your picture a title. Write two or three sentences about your picture.

_____

_____
_____
_____
_____

WRITE ABOUT IT!

You have just completed an unfinished picture. Your picture was probably very different from other students' pictures. Now try an unfinished **story**. Look at the picture. Write about this person in the picture by finishing the following sentences:

His name is _____. He is _____ years old, and he works in a _____. His occupation is _____. This man lives in _____ with his _____ and his _____. Every day he likes to

_____.

Two things he really doesn't like are _____ and _____.

Today he is doing something unusual. He is _____

_____

Yesterday he _____ and he felt _____ about it.

Tomorrow he will probably _____

_____

He is a very _____ man.

When you have finished writing, sit down in groups of four and compare your story with your partners' stories. Are they similar or very different? Share your stories with the whole class.

The Book

You have found a wonderful book. (It can be a *real* book or *any* book you'd like.) It tells you very important things that you want to know. Draw a picture of this wonderful book.

WRITE ABOUT YOUR DRAWING

What is the title of this book? What kind of important information does this book give you? How can it help you?

_____

_____

_____

_____

_____

Share your drawing and your sentences with your classmates. Tell them more about your book.

BRAINSTORM!

1. Sit down in groups of four. Look at the list of books below. They are all **personal** "how to" books—they tell you **how to** do things. Take three minutes working alone to put the books in order according to importance. Write numbers 1 through 10 next to the book titles.

_____ How to Stay Healthy

_____ How to Clean Your House and Keep It Clean

_____ How to Keep Peace With Your Neighbors

_____ How to Save Money

_____ How to Find a Good Husband or Wife

_____ How to Protect Your House and Possessions

_____ How to Fix Your Own Car

_____ How to Get Rich Quickly

_____ How to Find a Job You Like

_____ How to Have Good and Happy Children

After three minutes compare your list with those in your group. Try to decide together what the group's five most important books are.

2. Now look together at the list of books below. These are "how to" books, too. Work alone for three minutes. Choose what you think would be the four **most valuable** books to have and mark an "X" by them.

_____ How to End World Hunger

_____ How to Stop War

_____ How to Live Forever

_____ How to Give All Human Beings a Basic Education

_____ How to Stop Use of Dangerous Drugs

_____ How to End Crime in Our Neighborhoods

_____ How to Prevent Child Abuse

_____ How to End Unemployment

_____ How to Ensure Equal Rights for Women

_____ How to Protect Our Earth from Pollution

Share with your group what you think the four most valuable and necessary books would be. Discuss your lists with the whole class and try to decide together which are the **two** books most needed for the world today. If you can not agree, take a vote.

The Machine

Machines can do amazing things for us. They can help us in many ways. Work with a partner. On this paper, draw together a very special new machine that is very helpful to you both. It can do anything you want it to do. Be sure that this machine has many buttons and switches and springs and wheels that you can push and turn.

Button

Switch

Spring

Wheel

WRITE ABOUT YOUR DRAWING

What can your machine do? What happens when you push the button or turn the wheels or move the switches? What is the name of your machine?

_____

_____

_____

_____

_____

Share your drawing and writing with your classmates. Tell more about your machine.

BRAINSTORM!

Sit down in groups of four. In our homes we have many machines and appliances that run on electricity. Some of them work for us. Some of them are for recreation or fun. With your partners, brainstorm a list of the electrical items **you have in your four homes right now**. Decide which are for fun and entertainment and which ones are working machines or appliances.

FOR WORK	FOR ENTERTAINMENT
1. _____	1. _____
2. _____	2. _____
3. _____	3. _____
4. _____	4. _____
5. _____	5. _____
6. _____	6. _____
7. _____	7. _____
8. _____	8. _____
9. _____	9. _____
10. _____	10. _____
11. _____	11. _____
12. _____	12. _____
13. _____	13. _____
14. _____	14. _____
15. _____	15. _____

When you have finished your list, look at it carefully. Work alone for two minutes to cross out all the electrical items you have now that you **could live without**. Make circles around only six items that you **have to keep**.

After two minutes, take turns in your group to share the six items you feel you, personally, really need. Share your "needed" list with the whole class. The teacher will write the "needed" items that are common to the entire group on the board. If there are more than six items on the board, see if your group can decide together on **only six** for the entire group by discussing and voting.

Silent Partner

Sit down with one partner. Do not speak to each other. You will draw a picture together *without speaking to each other*. Make a line anywhere on the paper to begin the picture. Your partner will add a line to your line. Take turns adding pieces to the picture until you think it is finished.

WRITE ABOUT YOUR PICTURE

Talk to your partner about the picture you have drawn. Decide on a title for your drawing and write it here.

_____

_____

Share your drawing and title with your classmates. They may ask you questions about your drawing.

WRITE ABOUT IT!

Look carefully at the picture you and your partner drew together. Write your name on line **a)** below, and your partner's name on line **b)**. Write the title of your drawing on line **c)**. Work alone. Finish this story:

Yesterday was a rainy day and Larry didn't have to work or go to school. He was bored and couldn't find anything interesting to do. He decided to go to the new art gallery that had opened in town this week. The gallery had a special show of artwork by two of the most famous and talented new artists in town, **a)** _____ and **b)** _____.

The gallery was full of admiring art lovers. And I'm not surprised! Larry was amazed at the strange and wonderful pen and pencil drawings hanging on the walls. They were fabulous works of art! One drawing in particular fascinated him. It was titled:

      c) _____

In this fabulous drawing he saw _____

_____

_____

_____

_____

_____

As he looked at the drawing he felt _____
and thought _____.

He wanted very much to buy the drawing because _____

_____

_____.

Unfortunately, he told me later that he didn't buy the drawing after all because _____

_____.

When you have finished writing, compare your story with your partner's story. Are they similar or very different? Share your stories with the whole class or in small groups.

DRAWING OUT © 1992 by Prentice-Hall, Inc.
Permission granted to reproduce for classroom use.

The Frimpled Scloopf

In this bag is a frimpled scloopf. You can't see it, but it is in there. Draw a picture of what *you* think a frimpled scloopf looks like. Is it an animal? A machine? Something to wear? Is it something to eat? Guess!

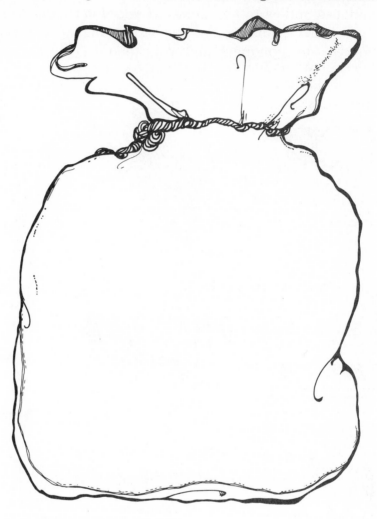

WRITE ABOUT YOUR DRAWING

What is a frimpled scloopf? What does it look like? What is it for or what does it do?

_____

_____

_____

_____

_____

Share your drawing and writing with your classmates. Tell more about the frimpled scloopf. Choose which drawing in the class is the best idea for a frimpled scloopf.

BRAINSTORM!

Sit down in groups of four. Look at the 12 pictures below. Do you know the names of these things in English? If you do, teach your group how to pronounce and write the names. If you don't know the name in English, do you know the names in your native language? If you do, teach your group how to pronounce and write them in your native language!

When all pictures are labeled, share your ideas orally with the whole class to see how you did.

Creatures from the Planet Pring-Lif

Look at the picture. This is the planet Pring-lif. On this planet, there are no human beings. Strange-looking creatures live on this planet. They have more than two eyes, more than one nose, and more than two legs. They are many different colors. They are friendly creatures. Draw a picture of a creature from the planet Pring-lif. Give it a name.

Name:

When you have finished your drawing, sit down in groups of six. Show your creature to your group and say its name. **Describe** your creature to your group members.

WRITE ABOUT IT!

Look at the creature from the planet Pring-lif that you have drawn. Answer the following questions:

What is the creature's name? _____

Is it a male or female? _____

What does it look like? _____

_____

_____

_____

_____

_____

_____

_____

What does this creature eat? _____

Where does it sleep? _____

Does it live alone or with others? _____

How many years does this creature live? _____

Does this creature have a language? _____

If this creature has a language, write a sentence in that language. _____

_____

_____

_____

When you have finished writing, sit down in groups of four. Show your creature to your group. Say its name and share your description orally. Decide together which creature you like the best in your group. The teacher will ask for volunteers to show and describe their creatures to the whole class.

The Quilp and the Toodee

On the top of this hill are a quilp and a toodee. They are having an interesting conversation. Work with a partner. You draw a quilp and your partner will draw a toodee. They are looking at each other. (You will have to *guess* what they look like.)

WRITE ABOUT YOUR DRAWING

Take turns with your partner and write an interesting conversation between the toodee and the quilp in the balloons.

Share your drawing and conversations with your classmates.

Choose the best picture in the class for first prize.

WRITE ABOUT IT!

Sit down with a partner. You have drawn a toodee and a quilp. Now look at these three creatures. They are not toodees or quilps. Working with your partner, give each creature a name. Answer some questions about each creature. Where does it live? What does it eat? What does it do? What noise does it make? Invent any story you like.

1. This is a _____.
   It lives _____ and it
   eats _____.
   It _____
   It makes a noise like _____

2. This is a _____.
   It lives _____ and it
   eats _____.
   It _____
   It makes a noise like _____

3. This is a _____.
   It lives _____ and it
   eats _____.
   It likes _____.
   It makes a noise like _____

When you have finished your writing, sit down in groups of four and read about your creatures. The teacher will ask some partners to read about their creatures in front of the class.

UNIT **7**

CONSTRUCTIONS AND PROJECTS

The 17 communication activities in this section **require no reproducible handouts**. They are, for the most part, "hands-on," manipulative activities that require students to draw, cut, paste, tear up magazines, share materials, and, in some cases, create large, whole-class projects. Complete instructions are provided to the teacher for each activity.

1. ALL ABOUT ME COLLAGE

Give each student a couple of magazines. Have them search through the magazines to find pictures of things they like or have an interest in, pictures of things they have or things they can do—anything that they can relate to themselves or their lives. They may also cut out large-print words and phrases. Give them large pieces of construction paper to glue their pictures on to form a personal collage. Ask them to write their names on their collages in large letters and label any pictures they want to label. During the searching, cutting, and pasting, circulate around the room asking questions of the students and making comments about their selections. Encourage interaction among the students during this activity. When all have completed their collages, form groups of four or five and have students take turns showing group members their work and asking questions of each other. If possible, display their work for a few days on the bulletin board. You may want to expand this activity into a writing assignment, asking students to write a number of sentences about the items on their collage.

2. USA COLLAGE

Have students form groups of four. Give each group a large piece of chart paper or butcher paper, some glue, scissors, and a stack of old magazines. Ask them to go through the magazines to look for pictures and words that show "United States culture"—or things that show what the rest of the world thinks about the United States. Ask them to cut out these items and words and glue them up on the chart paper as a USA culture collage. As students are working, circulate around the room from group to group asking questions, commenting on their choices and responding to their requests for assistance. When each group has completed their collage, each student is to write a paragraph about the collage. These writings can be shared orally with their group and/or with the whole class. If possible, display the collages with the writings in the classroom or in the hallways for others to comment on.

3. FIVE-PICTURE STORIES

Have students form groups of five. Give each student an old magazine. Each student finds one picture, tears it out, and puts it in the center of the table. The group members then consider the five pictures and arrange them in some order to tell a story that includes all five pictures. The story should be plotted orally with ideas coming from each student in the group. When they have their story line, each student will be responsible for the telling of one part of the story orally (and in writing, if you want to assign it). Have them glue their pictures on construction paper in the same sequence that they appear in the story and practice telling their parts in their groups. Circulate around the room during this activity to encourage and stimulate their participation. Have each group tell their story to the entire class on a voluntary basis. Some may feel comfortable sharing in the smaller group only.

4. PICTURE DIALOGUES

Have students sit down with one partner. Give each pair a couple of magazines. Have them search for a picture with two people in it. Have them cut out the picture of the two people and paste it on construction paper. The partners will write a dialogue between the two people in the picture with each student taking the role of one of the people depicted in the picture. When they have composed their dialogue and you have checked it, ask them to copy it neatly and glue it above the picture. They may read these aloud in small groups or post them on the bulletin board or hallways for others to read and comment on.

5. PICTURE DICTIONARY POSTERS

Beginning level students may work in groups of three, pulling pictures out of magazines—pictures of objects they *know* the names of or *want to know* the names of. Have them paste pictures on large pieces of construction paper and label those they know how to spell. If they **don't** know the name of an item, they must ask at least two other people in the class before they ask you. This is an excellent way to practice, "Excuse me, please, how do you say this (spell this) in English?" in a real context. When time is up or when most have finished their project, ask them to sit in groups of six or eight to share their posters with each other—saying and repeating words for each other. Each student becomes a "teacher" using his or her own self-made teaching materials. If possible, display these posters on the wall.

6. WORD MURALS

Tack up a large piece of butcher paper on the wall to be left up for several weeks. Title it "Words We Already Know." Have students sit in pairs and give them two or three magazines each. Have them search for large-print words from advertisements—words that they know and can pronounce. Do this for about ten minutes a day. Have them cut out the recognized words and tape or glue them to the mural. Be sure to move about the classroom during this activity so that you can encourage and inspire! We guarantee that students will spend a lot of independent time going over the words on the mural—those who arrive early for class, those who complete writing assignments early, during coffee break, and so on. You will also notice that students will stand around in groups or pairs quizzing and challenging each other to decode and define the words on the mural.

7. COOPERATIVE MURALS

Tack a large piece of butcher paper to the wall. Prepare slips of paper with concrete nouns written on them, enough for two per student in the class plus about ten extra in case someone is fast and needs three! The words should be for the most part known vocabulary—plate, table, car,

DRAWING OUT © 1992 by Prentice-Hall, Inc.
Permission granted to reproduce for classroom use.

chicken, jacket, sun, fish, water, shoe, skates, and similar words. Give each student a couple of crayons. Each student pulls one word from the box. All students go to the butcher paper at one time and begin drawing the item that is on their slip of paper. Ask them to watch each other and try to put their drawings together. The one with the *plate* might want to put it on the *table*. The one with the *bird* might want to put it in the *tree*, and so forth. When they have done one drawing they should come and get another word. When the "mural" is complete, open it up to the whole group to make oral statements about the mural. Use it as a writing stimulus as well. Leave it up for a few days for comments and musing.

8. BUILDING MACHINE-MEN (EMPHASIZING COLOR AND MEASUREMENT)

Show your students a poster of the machine-man (see page 126). Tell them that you would like them to build exactly the same machine-man working together in small groups. The first group to finish will win a prize!

Give each group the following handout:

ASSIGNMENT HANDOUT:

1. Cut one 2 inch square from white paper and color it yellow.
2. Cut two $\frac{1}{2}$ inch squares from red construction paper.
3. Cut one $\frac{1}{4}$ inch square from purple construction paper.
4. Cut one $\frac{1}{2}$ inch by 1 inch rectangle from red construction paper.
5. Assemble items 1, 2, 3, and 4 to form the machine-man's head.
6. Cut one rectangle 4 inches by 6 inches from blue construction paper.
7. Cut six $\frac{1}{2}$ inch squares from orange construction paper.
8. Assemble items 6 and 7 for the machine-man's body.
9. Cut two $1\frac{1}{2}$ inch by 3 inch rectangles from black paper.
10. Cut two $1\frac{3}{4}$ inch by 4 inch rectangles from black paper.
11. Assemble items 8 and 9 to form the machine-man's arms and legs.
12. Cut two 1 inch by $2\frac{1}{2}$ inch rectangles from pink paper.
13. Assemble item 12 to form machine-man's feet.
14. Glue all pieces to your poster to form your machine-man so that it looks exactly like the one I have made.

Rules for putting together the machine-man: Only one step of the assignment can be done at a time. Each step must be completed before the next one is begun. Each assignment must be checked as it is completed by the teacher before going on to the next step. All colors and measurements must be exact. Only one person from each group may come up to the checking table at one time. Only enough material for one assignment step may be taken from the main table at one time. The first group to satisfactorily complete the machine-man wins!

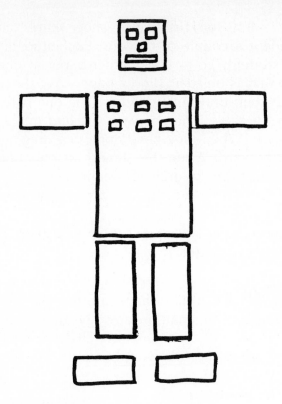

9. CLOTHING AND COLORS

Give each student a piece of 8 by 10 inch plain paper and a handful of crayons. Have them fold their paper into nine squares of equal size, then open out the paper so that they have a grid on which to draw. Ask a student to call out an article of clothing, such as "jacket." All students will draw with a crayon that article of clothing in the first square. Continue getting suggestions from the class and allowing a short time for each drawing until the nine squares are filled. **Important:** be sure to have students change colors after each drawing! From the front of the class, draw from a prepared stack of 3 by 5 cards that have an article of clothing and its color written on the back side, for example: **yellow shoes, blue tie, green shirt, red pants,** and so on. As you draw the card, ask "Who has a **purple skirt?**" "Who has an **orange sock?**" The students look at their drawings, and anyone who has the article of clothing **in the right color** wins a prize (chocolate kisses? free cup of coffee?).

These drawings can now be used for pair practice. Set up some sort of short, easy dialogue that works well for clothes and colors, such as:

STUDENT 1: Do you have a **jacket?**
STUDENT 2: Yes, I do. It's right here.
STUDENT 1: Oh. It's **purple.** Mine is **red.**
STUDENT 2: Yes, I see.

Have them go through this dialogue several times, taking turns and substituting the clothing and colors on their papers. While they are

DRAWING OUT © 1992 by Prentice-Hall, Inc.
Permission granted to reproduce for classroom use.

practicing, go around and listen to the pairs to find out who needs help with pronunciation. Talk with them encouragingly about their drawings.

10. FABRIC AND FORM

Bring small samples of fabric to class—all fibers and patterns and colors. You will need several swatches of each fabric. Place all samples in the middle of the room on a desk or table. Have students form groups of three or four. Give each group a handout that asks them to find on the table pieces of striped blue and green, polka-dot, and yellow cotton, flower-print wool, and so forth. One person from each group will come up to the center table and take a fabric sample for the group. Then the group will glue it to a piece of poster board and label it. Students will take turns going to the table for their group until their assignment is completed. When all groups are finished, return to the larger group and discuss the following questions:

A. Do you agree with the labels on the samples on all the posters?
B. What clothing articles would you make from this fabric?
C. Do you have any clothing made from these samples?
D. Does anyone in the class have on clothing now made from these samples?
E. How would you describe _____'s clothing?

11. WHO'S WEARING WHAT?

Have each student find a partner and give each pair catalogues or magazines, paper, glue, and scissors. Ask each pair to look through the books and select clothing for one person to wear—shoes, shirt, pants, socks, jacket, hat, and so on. Have them glue these to a piece of paper and write descriptions of the clothing. (This is a good follow-up activity for Fabric and Form.)

Ask each pair to share their selections and descriptions in front of the class and discuss any new vocabulary that comes up. After each pair has presented their work, place all clothing pictures in a row on the chalkboard. Give them a number. Place the descriptions on a table in mixed-up order. Have the students match up pictures and descriptions.

12. COLORS AND OBJECTS

Give each student a piece of 8 by 10 inch paper and a crayon or felt pen. Everyone should have the same color. Have them fold their paper into nine equal squares, then open it out so that they have a grid on which to draw. If their color is red, ask them to think of ten things that are sometimes or always red and draw one in each square. Give them no more than ten minutes and remind them when time is half up. From a stack of prepared 3 by 5 cards that have the name of something red on the back side, call out one card at a time and have the students make an "X" on that object if it is on their paper. (Examples might be: apple, lips, strawberry, radish, watermelon, shirt, fingernails, roses, cars, chile, and books.) The first person to "X" out all his or her squares wins a prize.

This grid of drawings may also be used for pair practice. Devise some sort of short dialogue that can be carried out with the drawings to reinforce current grammar items from your lesson plan. One example might be:

STUDENT 1: What's that thing?
STUDENT 2: It's **an apple!** Do you have **an apple,** too?
STUDENT 1: Yes, I do, too. (No, I don't.)

Have them go through this dialogue several times, using their papers as cues for the substitutions. Let them change partners and roles. While they are doing this, you can go around and listen to see who needs help with pronunciation and other matters. Be sure to comment on their drawings!

13. TRANSPORTATION

Give students nine pieces of paper each (about 3 by 3 inch scraps) and crayons. Tell them to draw the following—one on each piece of paper: bus, train, car, bicycle, taxi, airplane, motorcycle, ship, and subway. When all of the drawings are complete, remind them of the following directional signals: over, under, next to, on the right, on the left. Ask them to listen carefully as you give them directions and to do what you ask. Your directions will be something like, "Pick up the train and put it next to the bus, on the right side. Pick up the taxi and put it over the bus. Pick up the bicycle and put it under the train." (Follow your own instructions on your own desk, so that you can keep track!) You may have to go through this activity two times before everyone gets the idea. (They can watch each other—there is no such thing as cheating in this activity!) If almost everyone seems to be following, then try the next variation.

Put students in pairs. Give each pair a manila file folder to set on edge between them to act as a barrier. Each pair should be able to see each other's faces but not their partner's hands or slips of paper! Now have them go through the same "follow my instructions" activity with one partner dictating, the other acting. When each pair is finished, have them compare papers with their partner to see if they are in the same position. Then have them do it again, switching roles.

This listening comprehension/dictation activity may be done, of course, with any vocabulary category. The students never seem to tire of the format, as long as the content is new!

DRAWING OUT © 1992 by Prentice-Hall, Inc.
Permission granted to reproduce for classroom use.

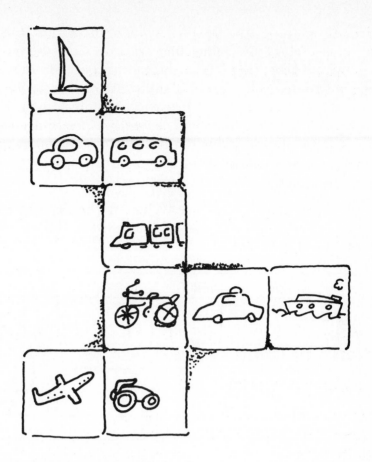

14. FOOD AND DRINK BINGO

Give each student a ditto sheet with a grid of 25 squares on it such as is used for any bingo game. In these squares have your students quickly sketch things to eat or drink and label them, for example: beer, soup, coffee, carrots, bananas, apples, milk, cake. They will need at least 15 minutes to complete the drawings, and depending on their level, more time and help with the writing. Have them help each other with spelling and ideas. This is also very valuable use of time! When each student is finished (and you may have to give special assistance to some), play bingo with these papers. You call out names of foods and drinks and the first three who get bingo win a prize.

It is good to keep in mind that it is not only the game that is valid here, but the **preparation** for the game—the visual and kinesthetic reinforcement of vocabulary, the quiet time, the peer help.

15. BUILDINGS, PLACES, AND OCCUPATIONS

Prepare a large piece of butcher paper before class (approximately 3 by 8 feet) with a map such as that shown below. Show it to your students and tell them that we are going to put the buildings and people in the town on it. Pass out small slips of paper with names of occupations (police officer, teacher, doctor, mechanic, dishwasher, waitress, and others) and places to go (drugstore, market, garage, restaurant, bus station, school, and others). Hand out paper and crayons. Give them about ten minutes to draw and label pictures according to their slip of paper. As they finish, they can come up to the map and paste their drawings on the map on the street they choose. (Or, if it is on a bulletin board, they can use pins.) It is a good idea to scale their drawing paper to a good size to fit the map, so that you don't have a post office that takes up three blocks or a miniature supermarket! When the town is finished, you can use it as a focus for practice in asking directions:

STUDENT 1: Excuse me, please. Where is the department store?
STUDENT 2: It's on the corner of Main Street and First Avenue.
STUDENT 1: Thank you.

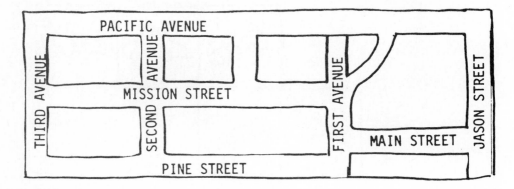

16. ADJECTIVES AND OPPOSITES

Give your students a piece of 8 by 10 inch plain paper and some crayons or markers. Ask them to fold their paper into nine equal spaces and then open it out to produce a grid on which to draw. Ask them to quickly draw what you dictate and write as well: a fat cat, an old shoe, a tall tree, a big piece of cake, a woman with curly hair, a rich man, an open box, a long snake, a happy student. When they are finished, have them turn their papers over and draw the **opposites**.

As they are completing this part, go around and have students show you their work and read for you. As an aid to those who don't write or spell well yet, have students who finish first write possible answers on the chalkboards or go around offering their help.

17. PREPOSITIONS

Before class, prepare a silly description of an impossible scene. Give the students pieces of plain paper and crayons and have them draw as you read the description. Be sure to use a lot of prepositions of place: "A short man with long, long hair is standing next to a bus with a flat tire. There are three chickens sitting on top of the bus. A beautiful young woman wearing shorts is waiting on the corner in front of the barber shop. She has a tennis racket in her hand and a baseball cap on her head. Next to the barbershop, on the left, is a dog eating an ice-cream cone . . ." and so on.

DRAWING OUT © 1992 by Prentice-Hall, Inc.
Permission granted to reproduce for classroom use.